Final Campaigns
of the Civil War

DISCARD

Cinci Stowell

CRABTREE
Publishing Company
www.crabtreebooks.com

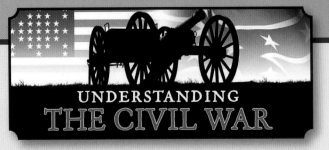

UNDERSTANDING THE CIVIL WAR

Author: Cinci Stowell
Publishing plan research and development:
 Sean Charlebois, Reagan Miller
 Crabtree Publishing Company
Editors: Mark Cheatham, Kirsten Holm, Lynn Peppas
Proofreader: Wendy Scavuzzo
Editorial director: Kathy Middleton
Production coordinator: Shivi Sharma
Creative director: Arka Roy Chaudhary
Design: Sandy Kent
Cover design: Samara Parent
Photo research: Iti Shrotriya
Maps: Paul Brinkdopke
Production coordinator: Margaret Amy Salter
Prepress technician: Margaret Amy Salter
Print coordinator: Katherine Berti

Written, developed, and produced by Planman Technologies

Photographs and Reproductions
Front cover © Bettmann/CORBIS; Title Page (p. 1): Universal History Archive/Photolibrary (top); Library of Congress; Table of Contents (p. 3): Chapter 1: Library of Congress; Chapter 2: Library of Congress; Chapter 3: Eon Images; Chapter 4: Library of Congress; Chapter 5: Corbis; Chapter Opener image (pp. 5, 13, 21, 26, 34): Sheridan/PoodlesRock/Corbis
Corbis, pp. 4, 12, 19 (bottom), 40; Eon Images, p. 23; Library of Congress, pp. 6, 8, 14, 15, 17, 19 (top), 22, 24, 30, 32, 33, 35, 36, 37, 43; North Wind Picture Archives / Alamy, p. 16; Universal History Archive/Photolibrary, p. 29

Front cover: An illustration depicts the destruction in Georgia by Union soldiers under the command of General William Tecumseh Sherman.
Back cover (background): A military map of the United States from 1862 showing forts and military posts.
Back cover (logo): A civil war era cannon stands in front of the flag from Fort Sumter.
Title page (top): An illustration by Felix Octavius Carr Darley shows Sherman's March to the Sea.
Title page (bottom): Ruined buildings in Charleston, South Carolina

Library and Archives Canada Cataloguing in Publication

Stowell, Cinci
 Final campaigns of the Civil War / Cinci Stowell.

(Understanding the Civil War)
Includes index.
Issued also in electronic formats.
ISBN 978-0-7787-5339-1 (bound).--ISBN 978-0-7787-5356-8 (pbk.)

 1. United States--History--Civil War, 1861-1865--Campaigns--Juvenile literature. I. Title. II. Series: Understanding the Civil War

E470.S76 2011   j973.7'3   C2011-907482-6

Library of Congress Cataloging-in-Publication Data

Stowell, Cinci, 1950-
 Final campaigns of the Civil War / Cinci Stowell.
  p. cm. -- (Understanding the Civil War)
 Includes index.
 ISBN 978-0-7787-5339-1 (reinforced library binding : alk. paper) --
ISBN 978-0-7787-5356-8 (pbk. : alk. paper) -- ISBN 978-1-4271-9938-6
(electronic pdf) -- ISBN 978-1-4271-9947-8 (electronic html)
 1. United States--History--Civil War, 1861-1865--Juvenile literature. 2.
United States--History--Civil War, 1861-1865--Campaigns--Juvenile
literature. I. Title.
 E468.S885 2011
 973.7'37--dc23
                                        2011045081

Crabtree Publishing Company

www.crabtreebooks.com   1-800-387-7650

Printed in the U.S.A./112011/JA20111018

Published in Canada
Crabtree Publishing
616 Welland Ave.
St. Catharines, Ontario
L2M 5V6

Published in the United States
Crabtree Publishing
PMB 59051
350 Fifth Avenue, 59th Floor
New York, New York 10118

Published in the United Kingdom
Crabtree Publishing
Maritime House
Basin Road North, Hove
BN41 1WR

Published in Australia
Crabtree Publishing
3 Charles Street
Coburg North
VIC 3058

TABLE *of* CONTENTS

1

The Final Phase Begins

State of the War | Grant Takes Command
The Coordinated Advances Begin | The Overland
Campaign | Sherman Marches Toward Atlanta

5

2

Hope Fades for the South

The Election Looms | Siege of Petersburg
The Shenandoah Valley | Mobile Bay
The Fall of Atlanta | Lincoln Wins Reelection

13

3

The Tennessee Campaign

The Importance of Chattanooga
Hood and Sherman Part Ways | Spring Hill | The Battle
of Franklin | The Battle of Nashville

21

4

Sherman's Southern Campaign

Sherman's March to the Sea
The March Begins | Sherman in the Carolinas
Effects of Sherman's Campaign

26

5

The Civil War Ends

The Noose Tightens on Petersburg | Fall of Richmond
Appomattox Campaign | Surrender at Appomattox Court
House | The End of the Confederacy | Assassination of
Abraham Lincoln | Summary of the Final Campaigns
Effects of the Civil War

34

Glossary, 45 | More Information, 47 | Index, 48

> *I felt like anything rather than rejoicing at the downfall of a foe who had fought so long and valiantly, and had suffered so much for a cause, though that cause was, I believe, one of the worst for which a people ever fought. . . .”*
>
> —General Ulysses S. Grant on the surrender of General Lee's Army of Northern Virginia at Appomattox Court House, Virginia, April 9, 1865

General Robert E. Lee surrenders at Appomattox Court House, Virginia, April 9, 1865.

The Final Phase Begins

By late 1863, the Civil War was still raging. As Union and Confederate forces continued to battle, the losses on both sides mounted. **Civilians** on both sides were tired of the war and disheartened by the staggering loss of life. The losses were taking a toll on the political situation as well. Union victories in a few key battles, however, were finally beginning to turn the tide of the war.

State of the War

In the East, the Union victory at Gettysburg on July 3, 1863, proved to be a critical turning point. In the West, the Union's long **siege** of Vicksburg finally ended July 4, 1863. The South's surrender at Vicksburg gave the North control of the **vital** Mississippi River. Supplies could now be shipped freely along this major waterway to Union troops.

Chattanooga, Tennessee, located on the border with Georgia, was known as "the Gateway to the Deep South." This city was also an important railroad center. Chattanooga fell to the North in November 1863. This victory gave the North a base from which to transport supplies.

As the war dragged into its fourth year, **despair** settled over the people of the South. Soldiers and civilians faced food shortages. Heavy losses in battle had weakened their

Major Events
1864

March
Grant becomes general-in-chief

April
Union defeated at Mansfield

May
Grant's Overland Campaign begins
Union defeated at New Market

July
Sherman reaches Atlanta

> *…gloom and unspoken despondency [despair] hang like a pall [cloth covering a coffin] everywhere.*
>
> —Diary of Mary Chesnut, a citizen of South Carolina, December 1863

armies. By the spring of 1864, Confederate forces numbered less than half of Union forces. Southerners could see the end coming, and it terrified them.

Grant Takes Command

President Abraham Lincoln was impressed with Ulysses S. Grant. As chief of Union forces west of the Appalachians, Grant had led Union troops to victory at Vicksburg and at Chattanooga. President Lincoln believed he had found the strong leader he was looking for. In March 1864, Lincoln **promoted** Grant to general-in-chief of the Armies of the United States. Grant was now in command of all Union forces.

Grant's Coordinated Strategy

A **strategy** is a plan or method for reaching a goal. In the past, each Union army had acted on its own. Grant's strategy was to **coordinate** the movements of the Union armies. Working together instead of individually, the Union armies would defeat the Confederacy. In the spring of 1864, Grant's plan was to **engage** each Confederate army at the same time. This would keep one Confederate army from coming to the aid of another.

General George Meade led the Union Army of the Potomac. Grant told Meade to follow Robert E. Lee's Confederate Army of Northern Virginia wherever it went. General William Tecumseh Sherman took Grant's place as chief of the Union forces in the West. Grant told Sherman to move against the army of Joseph Johnston.

Policy of Destruction

Part of Grant's strategy was to destroy the South's war **resources**. All armies need food, weapons, clothing, shoes, and other supplies. They also need ways to transport these **necessities** to the troops. Grant instructed his generals to destroy roads, railroads, bridges, and tunnels as they marched. They would also destroy factories and shipyards that made the weapons of war.

Union troops often took crops and farm animals they encountered along the way. This strategy took food away from Confederate soldiers and civilians.

General Ulysses
S. Grant

The South's Strategy

In November 1864, President Lincoln ran for reelection. Public opinion about the war helped determine the outcome of the election. Southern leaders knew that many people in the North were growing weary of war. If Confederate forces could hold out until the election, Lincoln might lose. The new president might favor **independence** for the South in exchange for peace.

General Grant understood the importance of the election as well. He knew he had to produce major Union victories before November. Then voters might support Lincoln and the war through to final victory.

> *[Whether Lincoln] shall ever be elected or not depends upon … the battlefields of 1864.*
>
> —Prediction in a Georgia newspaper

The Coordinated Advances Begin

Grant put his plan into action in May 1864. Five Union armies were to move against different Confederate armies at the same time. The Union armies were led by Nathaniel Banks, Benjamin Butler, Franz Sigel, Sherman, and Meade. At first, this battle plan did not work out well for Union forces.

The Red River Campaign

Grant's plan called for the army led by Nathaniel Banks to capture Mobile, Alabama. After that, Banks was supposed to halt the movement of Confederate forces in Alabama. This would prevent the Alabama army from coming to the aid of Johnston's forces in Georgia. Johnston would then have to fight Sherman without help.

In April 1864, Banks advanced along the Red River in Louisiana. A fleet of gunboats under the command of David Dixon Porter supported Banks's army. Their target was Shreveport, the Confederate capital of Louisiana. Shreveport was also home to several war industries. Union troops were expected to take or destroy cotton as they marched. Cotton was the major source of income for the South.

The Confederates **routed** the Union army at Mansfield, south of Shreveport. The Union troops tried to retreat. The Red River had become so shallow that the gunboats could not pass. Banks's army was trapped. Only the quick thinking of a junior officer, Joseph Bailey, saved the soldiers. Bailey built small dams to raise the water level enough to float the boats through the rapids.

The Union forces escaped, but Banks failed in his mission. Confederate forces from Alabama were able to **reinforce** Johnston's army.

The Bermuda Hundred

In Virginia, Grant's plan called for three Union armies to advance at the same time. Their goal was to capture Richmond, Virginia, which was the capital of the Confederacy. Grant would go with Meade's army to fight Lee's forces in northern Virginia. Meanwhile, Franz Sigel would take his army south through the Shenandoah Valley. Benjamin Butler's army was to advance north up the James River toward Richmond.

In early May 1864, Butler's forces moved up the James River. They landed on the Bermuda Hundred, an area between Richmond and Petersburg, Virginia. Butler's orders were to destroy the railroad tracks to prevent supplies from reaching Richmond. Then his troops would march on Richmond itself.

At the time, only a small number of Confederate troops defended Petersburg and Richmond. Lee could not help. His army was busy with Meade's Union forces in the north. Had Butler struck quickly, he might have crushed Richmond's weak defenses.

Instead, Butler advanced slowly. This allowed time for Confederate General P.G.T. Beauregard to arrive with reinforcements. Now the number of soldiers on each side was nearly equal. The Confederates drove Butler's forces back. Butler had missed his chance at glory.

The Battle of New Market

In the same month, early May 1864, Franz Sigel's forces advanced in the Shenandoah Valley. At New Market, Virginia, a smaller force of Confederates sent Sigel into retreat. This defeat was especially **humiliating** for Sigel. The Confederate force included 247 cadets, young men ages 15 to 17, from the Virginia Military Institute.

The Overland Campaign

The failure of Banks and Sigel dealt a blow to Grant's plans to capture Richmond. Still, Grant expected the main thrust in Virginia to come from the large Army of the Potomac. General George Meade headed

People in the War

Nathaniel P. Banks

Nathaniel Banks was not trained in warfare. He was a politician. He hoped to run for president in 1864. To win political support, he needed success on the battlefield. The Red River Campaign offered an opportunity. His many blunders in the field, however, ruined his hopes for high office. He was removed from command after his humiliating defeat in the Battle of Mansfield.

the army. Grant traveled with Meade, so Grant was really in charge. The series of battles between Grant and Lee in Virginia became known as the Overland Campaign.

The Wilderness

The Overland Campaign began May 5 in northern Virginia in an area of dense forest and thickets. This region of Virginia was called The Wilderness. Grant hoped to draw Lee's smaller force out into the open and destroy it. Lee knew better than to meet Grant in the open. Instead, Lee waited for the Union troops to move into the forest. Lee expected that, in the forest, the size difference of the armies would not matter as much.

The battle was intense. Soldiers could not move quickly through the thick forest. Smoke from musket fire filled the air, making it difficult to see. Exploding shells set the brush on fire. Three days of fierce fighting ended with no clear winner.

Unlike Union generals before him, Grant did not retreat. Instead, he ordered the Army of the Potomac to continue to advance south toward Richmond. This bold order raised the spirits of the soldiers.

About 28,000 soldiers were killed or wounded in the Battle of the Wilderness. However, Grant lost about 7,000 more men than Lee.

GRANT'S VIEW Grant knew that his army could withstand heavy losses. The North had more men than the South. Therefore, Grant was willing to accept greater losses to drain manpower from the smaller Confederate forces. The South was running out of time and men.

LEE'S VIEW On the other hand, Lee hoped that the Union's terrible losses would shock the people of the North. He hoped that, as a result, they might vote Lincoln out of office and end the war.

> *The woods were set on fire by the bursting shells…. The wounded who had not strength to move…were either suffocated or burned to death.*
>
> —Personal Memoirs of Ulysses S. Grant about the Battle of the Wilderness

Spotsylvania

After the Battle of the Wilderness, Grant's forces tried to advance on Richmond around Lee's **flank**. On May 8, the two great armies faced off again at Spotsylvania Court House. The Battle of Spotsylvania was

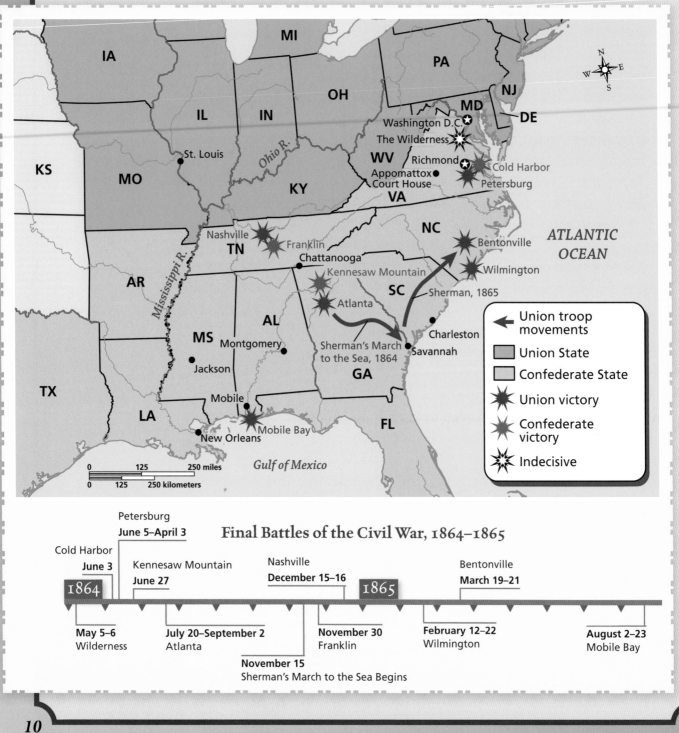

Final Battles of the Civil War, 1864–1865

Petersburg
June 5–April 3

Cold Harbor
June 3

Kennesaw Mountain
June 27

Nashville
December 15–16

Bentonville
March 19–21

1864

1865

May 5–6
Wilderness

July 20–September 2
Atlanta

November 30
Franklin

February 12–22
Wilmington

August 2–23
Mobile Bay

November 15
Sherman's March to the Sea Begins

actually a series of battles that lasted two weeks, from May 8 to May 21, 1864. Grant began with 110,000 men. Lee tried to hold off the Union advance with only 50,000 men.

The Confederate soldiers dug lines of trenches for defense. They spread logs and piled earth in front of the trenches to slow the advancing enemy.

On May 12, Union forces attacked the Confederates at a slight bend in the trenches. This bend would become known as the Bloody Angle. Furious **hand-to-hand** fighting continued for 18 hours. Still, Lee's forces managed to hold off the Union attack.

From May 5 through May 12, the Army of the Potomac suffered 32,000 **casualties**. The losses to the Army of Northern Virginia numbered 18,000. Yet even more bloodshed lay ahead.

> *I never expect to be fully believed when I tell what I saw of the horrors of Spotsylvania…*
>
> —A Union officer

Cold Harbor

Grant continued his advance south. Lee learned of Grant's movements and beat the Union forces to the North Anna River. They fought small battles as Grant pushed ever closer to Richmond.

By early June, Lee's army had dug in at Cold Harbor, Virginia. Reinforcements had swelled the ranks of both armies. Now 59,000 Confederate soldiers faced 109,000 Union soldiers. Grant thought that Lee's army was weak enough that he could attack the Confederate forces head-on. A win would give Union forces a clear path to Richmond.

Grant gave the order to attack at dawn on June 3, 1864. This was a deadly mistake that cost Grant's army about 7,000 men in one day of fighting. Lee's army lost fewer than 1,500. Still, Grant's forces pushed on toward their next target—Petersburg, Virginia.

> *I regret this assault more than any one I have ever ordered.*
>
> —Ulysses S. Grant, at the end of the battle at Cold Harbor

Sherman Marches Toward Atlanta

William Tecumseh Sherman's army in the West was the fifth prong of Grant's coordinated strategy. Sherman's orders were to break up the Confederate army commanded by Joseph Johnston. Grant told Sherman to "get into the interior of the enemy's country as far as you can, inflicting all the damage you can against their war resources."

General William Tecumseh Sherman

Along with the other armies in the coordinated effort, Sherman began his march in early May 1864. He left Chattanooga, Tennessee, with his sights set on Atlanta, Georgia. Atlanta was an important manufacturing center in the South. It was also a key railroad center.

During the first month of the campaign, Sherman tried to get around the side of Johnston's army. Each time, Johnston retreated and took up a strong position further into Georgia. They fought constant **skirmishes**, but no large battles. Confederate forces succeeded in slowing Sherman's advance, but they could not stop it.

By mid-July, Johnston had pulled back to Peachtree Creek, only four miles (6 km) from Atlanta. Confederate President Jefferson Davis was alarmed. He replaced Johnston with John Bell Hood.

Unlike the cautious Johnston, Hood was a bold fighter. Hood quickly attacked the larger Union army. Hood's decision to attack was a disaster for the South. In three battles over eight days, Hood lost 15,000 men. Sherman lost only 6,000. Sherman's army stood on Atlanta's doorstep. Despite these Union advances, the capture of Atlanta was still six long weeks away.

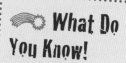 **What Do You Know!**

SHERMAN'S NECKTIES

As Sherman's troops marched south, they pulled up the rails from railroad tracks and heated them over a fire. When the rails were hot enough to bend, the soldiers wrapped them around trees. The twisted metal became known as Sherman's Neckties.

Hope Fades for the South

Grant's coordinated strategy had begun in the spring of 1864 with five Union armies advancing on the South at the same time. Confederate forces had, however, stopped the marches of Union forces under Banks, Butler, and Sigel. By late summer 1864, victory depended on the two main Union forces led by Grant and Sherman.

The Election Looms

The North would hold its presidential election in November, and its outcome depended on the war effort. By August, Grant's great Army of the Potomac had stalled outside Petersburg, Virginia. Sherman's army was battling Hood's Confederates, but Union forces had not succeeded in taking Atlanta.

Mood in the North

Northerners were becoming impatient. To them, Union troops seemed to be making little progress. The terrible losses suffered by Grant's army during the Overland Campaign shocked them. Many questioned whether the North could restore the Union through war. Northern voters wanted peace and an end to this long war.

Major Events

1864

June
Union siege of Petersburg begins

August
Union victory at Mobile Bay

September
Union occupies Atlanta

Sheridan plunders Shenandoah Valley

November
Lincoln wins reelection

> "
> *I am going to be beaten, and unless some great change takes place, badly beaten.*
>
> —President Abraham Lincoln, August 1864
> "

UNION AND LIBERTY!   AND   UNION AND SLAVERY!

This political cartoon from the election of 1864 contrasts the political views of Abraham Lincoln and George McClellan. Under Lincoln on the left is the motto "Union and Liberty!" Under McClellan is the motto "Union and Slavery!" A slave auction appears behind McClellan under a Confederate flag.

The Democratic party saw an opportunity to defeat Lincoln's bid for a second term. The Democrats chose George B. McClellan to run against Lincoln. McClellan wanted to end the war right away. He wanted to try to restore the Union by peaceful **negotiations** rather than armed conflict. To McClellan, peace was more important than restoring the Union.

With growing **discontent** among Northern voters, Lincoln expected to lose the election. His hopes for reelection—and for restoring the Union—were hinged on battlefield success.

Mood in the South

The situation looked even more bleak to Southerners during the August before the presidential election. Grant's army had dug in at Petersburg, just a few miles from Richmond, the Confederate capital. Atlanta was in danger of falling to Sherman.

McClellan's **platform** encouraged Southerners and gave them hope. Maybe they could win independence without winning the war. They just had to hold off Union forces until the November election.

Siege of Petersburg

After heavy losses at Cold Harbor, Grant's Army of the Potomac continued its advance. Instead of marching directly to Richmond, Grant directed his army toward Petersburg, just south of Richmond.

> *We must destroy this Army of Grant's before he gets to the James River [near Petersburg]. If he gets there it will become a siege and then it will be a mere question of time.*
>
> —Robert E. Lee to Jubal Early, late May 1864

Five railroads and several **plank roads** from Petersburg brought supplies to Richmond. If Grant could cut off these supply lines, Richmond could not hold out.

Earthworks

At Cold Harbor, Grant learned the difficulty of attacking an enemy that was firmly **entrenched**. Thousands of Union soldiers lost their lives when they charged the trenches. At Petersburg, Grant's army would again face these dreaded earthworks.

Earthworks, also called breastworks, were defenses built from earth. Soldiers dug trenches. In front of the trenches, they mounded earth over logs. To slow the attackers, the soldiers dug ditches in front of the mounds. The earthworks shielded the soldiers' bodies from enemy fire. Soldiers charging over open ground were fully exposed to gunfire. As a result, earthworks could help entrenched soldiers hold off the charges of a larger enemy force.

When the first Union troops reached Petersburg, they faced 10 miles (16 km) of earthworks. In front of the trenches were earth mounds 20 feet (6 m) thick and ditches 15 feet (5 m) deep.

The Siege of Petersburg

Instead of attacking, Grant decided to lay siege to Petersburg. His army could block most of the supplies headed for the city. Grant ordered his army to dig trenches. The Army of the Potomac settled in. They were determined to starve out the Confederates. Time, however, was on the side of the Confederates. The defenders of Petersburg had to hold on only four months until the election.

Earthworks at Petersburg, Virgina

Battle of the Crater

The Battle of the Crater

As the **stalemate** dragged on through July, frustration grew among the Union soldiers at Petersburg. One regiment from Pennsylvania contained coal miners who knew how to dig mine shafts. They proposed digging a tunnel under the Confederate line. They could then place explosives in the tunnel and blow a hole in the Confederate defenses. Their commander approved the plan.

The soldiers dug a tunnel more than 500 feet (152 m) long. They packed the tunnel with four tons of gunpowder. The resulting explosion killed dozens of Confederate soldiers above the tunnel.

Union troops rushed through the cleared section. The Confederate forces cut them down. A division of black soldiers followed the first wave of white soldiers into the gap. By this time, the Confederates had organized a **counterattack**. The black soldiers bore the full force of this assault. When the black soldiers tried to surrender, angry Confederate soldiers killed many of them.

This battle, known as the Battle of the Crater, cost the Union army 4,000 men. The Confederate army lost less than 2,000.

The Shenandoah Valley

In June 1864, Robert E. Lee made a bold move. To take the pressure off his army, he sent a force under General Jubal Early through the Shenandoah Valley of Virginia toward Washington, DC. Lee hoped that Grant would be forced to send some of his troops to defend Washington. This would weaken the Union forces facing Lee's army at Petersburg.

Lynchburg

After Franz Sigel's defeat at New Market in May, General David Hunter replaced Sigel. Hunter marched his Union troops into the Shenandoah Valley. He intended to capture the railroad center of Lynchburg, Virginia.

Jubal Early raced to the defense of Lynchburg. In June, Early sent Hunter's forces into retreat. Then Early's army continued the march north.

The Battle of Monocacy

Early's forces crossed the Potomac River into Maryland on July 6. On July 9, a small Union force under General Lew Wallace tried to stop Early's advance at the Monocacy River.

After learning about Early's advance, Grant rushed troops from Petersburg to defend Washington. Wallace's forces could not stop Early. They were able to delay the Confederates long enough, however, for Grant's troops to reach Washington. With the reinforcements, the Union defenders now outnumbered Early's forces. Seeing little chance to capture Washington, Early retreated into the Shenandoah Valley.

Sheridan Takes Charge in the Shenandoah

Taking soldiers from other Union armies, Grant created the new Army of the Shenandoah. On August 6, 1864, he placed Philip Sheridan in command. Grant gave Sheridan two orders. He should follow Jubal Early "to the death," and turn the Shenandoah into a "barren waste."

At Winchester, Virginia, Sheridan received reports that Lee had sent reinforcements to Early. When he learned that many Confederate troops had left, Sheridan decided to attack.

On September 19, Sheridan's army of 37,000 clashed with Early's force of only 15,000. In the Third Battle of Winchester, Early lost one-quarter of his army. He was forced to retreat 20 miles (32 km) to Fisher's Hill.

People in the War

Philip Sheridan

Abraham Lincoln once described Philip Sheridan as "a brown, chunky little chap, with...not enough neck to hang him." But to his troops, Sheridan was "Little Phil."

After the war, Sheridan served as a general on the Great Plains. As he blazed trails in Yellowstone National Park, he saw widespread slaughter of elk and buffalo. On a camping trip in the park with President Chester Arthur, Sheridan pushed for greater protection of the animals.

Total War

The Shenandoah Valley was called the "breadbasket of the Confederacy," and it was vital to the South. Its rich farmland produced much of the grain for Southern soldiers and civilians. Grant wanted to take this resource away from the Confederacy.

Sheridan continued to pursue Early. On September 22, the Confederate defense collapsed at Fisher's Hill. This opened the way for Sheridan to carry out Grant's second order. Sheridan would turn the upper Shenandoah Valley into a "barren waste."

Sheridan did not focus on military targets alone. His forces also destroyed homes and farms. This was **total war**. This new way of waging war did not spare civilian property. Armies destroyed everything in their path, including crops, barns, and farm equipment. The goal of total war was to create devastating hardship among the population. With no means of survival, the disheartened, financially ruined people might then push their leaders to surrender.

> *It is desirable that nothing should be left to invite the enemy to return. Take all provisions, forage [food] and stock [livestock] … such as cannot be consumed, destroy … If the war is to last another year, we want the Shenandoah Valley to remain a barren waste.*
>
> —Ulysses S. Grant's orders to Philip Sheridan, August 1864

The Burning

For nearly two weeks in September, Sheridan's men plundered 92 miles (148 km) of the Shenandoah Valley, from Winchester to Staunton. They burned barns filled with wheat and mills filled with flour. They took livestock and food. What they did not need, they burned. When they had finished, there was little of value left for the Confederacy. The people of the valley called this period of destruction *The Burning*.

Battle of Cedar Creek

In October, while Sheridan was away, Jubal Early made a last attempt to defeat the Army of the Shenandoah. His surprise attack at Cedar Creek nearly succeeded, but Sheridan returned just in time to rally his troops. The Union army nearly destroyed Early's army. The Confederates would never again control the Shenandoah Valley.

What Do You Know!

ARLINGTON NATIONAL CEMETERY
By the spring of 1864, the military cemeteries of Washington were already filled with Union dead. The site chosen for the new Union cemetery was the front lawn of Robert E. Lee's house in Arlington, Virginia. Lee's yard became Arlington National Cemetery.

Mobile Bay

While Union soldiers fought on land, the Union navy enforced a **blockade** along the southern coasts through much of the war. Union ships stopped food and supplies from getting to the Confederacy. The blockade also prevented the South from selling its cotton to other countries. The South desperately needed money from trade, especially from the sale of cotton, to continue the war. **Blockade runners**, however, could get through to some Southern ports. One such port was Mobile Bay, Alabama.

The North wanted to close Mobile Bay to blockade runners. On August 5, 1864, Admiral David Farragut boldly took his Union fleet of 18 ships into Mobile Bay. Two forts, Fort Morgan and Fort Gains, guarded the entrance to the bay. The Confederates also spread explosive mines, called torpedoes, in the water. They had left only a narrow passage free of mines so that blockade runners could get through. Unfortunately for Farragut, this passage ran directly under the guns of Fort Morgan.

As Farragut's fleet traveled through the passage, the Union **ironclad** ship *Tecumseh* struck a mine and sunk. Farragut's fleet stalled under the guns of the fort. To see above the smoke of battle, Farragut climbed a **mast** on his ship. He knew he had to direct his ship to the front of the fleet. To do this, he had to go through the mine field.

Farragut had tied himself to the mast to avoid falling if he were wounded. As an officer pointed out mines in front of his ship, Farragut uttered his famous reply, "Damn the torpedoes! Full speed ahead!"

People in the War

Admiral David Farragut

By the time David Farragut met Franklin Buchanan in Mobile Bay, Farragut had been in the navy for 51 years. He entered at age 8 because of an unlikely event. Farragut's father Jorge saved the life of an elderly man he found unconscious in a boat. That man turned out to be the father of David Porter, a captain in the U.S. Navy. To thank Jorge, Captain Porter offered to take his son to sea. The son, James Farragut, changed his name to David to honor his sponsor.

Farragut's fleet captured the Confederate ironclad ship *Tennessee* in Mobile Bay.

Farragut made it through the mine field and into the bay. The rest of his fleet followed. Confederate Admiral Franklin Buchanan and his ironclad ship *Tennessee* were waiting for him. The *Tennessee* and Farragut's ship *Hartford* steamed directly toward each other. The Union fleet fired furiously, disabling the ironclad. Knowing that the battle was lost, Buchanan surrendered.

Later, Union forces captured Fort Gaines and Fort Morgan. By August 23, the port was closed to the Confederacy. The victory raised the spirits of Northerners. This naval victory would also have significant political impact.

The Fall of Atlanta

> *We are going to be wiped off the earth.*
> —Diary of Mary Chesnut, after the fall of Atlanta

Through the first part of August, Sherman and Hood had been skirmishing around Atlanta, Georgia. On August 26, Sherman pulled his troops back. Hood's army celebrated. They thought Sherman was retreating. Instead, Sherman's troops marched south to cut roads and railroads that had been bringing food and supplies to Atlanta.

Hood attacked the Union forces at Jonesborough, but his soldiers failed to stop the Union advance. Sherman's counterattack devastated Hood's army. Hood retreated back into Atlanta and had his army destroy all military equipment to keep it from falling into enemy hands. On September 1, 1864, Hood evacuated Atlanta. The next day, the Union army marched in. Gloom fell over the South. Hope was all but gone.

Lincoln Wins Reelection

The fall of Atlanta was the miracle Lincoln needed. With the November election fast approaching, Union forces had delivered a great victory. Newspapers began to glorify the recent naval victory at Mobile Bay as well. More Union victories in the Shenandoah Valley soon followed.

The unfavorable public opinion toward the war and Lincoln quickly reversed. Northern voters could see that victory was at hand.

McClellan's platform stated that the war was a failure. His party called for immediate peace. The recent battlefield victories made this view unpopular. Lincoln won reelection, ensuring that the war would continue to final victory.

3 The Tennessee Campaign

The Union army of William Tecumseh Sherman had forced the Confederate troops out of Atlanta. Still, John Bell Hood's Army of Tennessee remained a dangerous force of 40,000.

The Importance of Chattanooga

The Union troops in Atlanta depended on supplies coming by railroad from Chattanooga. Hood planned to destroy the rail line that was bringing food and supplies to Sherman's forces in Atlanta.

Throughout the fall of 1864, Hood's soldiers tore up rail lines between Chattanooga and Atlanta. At first, Sherman sent troops to chase Hood. Sherman soon saw, however, that protecting rail lines could be an endless task. Sherman had a better idea.

Hood and Sherman Part Ways

Although Hood skirmished with Sherman's troops, he made little progress toward regaining Atlanta. In late November, Hood led his army into Tennessee. Hood's plan was to cut through Tennessee to Kentucky. There, he expected to pick up recruits for his army. He would then head into Virginia to join Lee against Grant.

Sherman prepared to march through Georgia. This plan worried Grant. He feared Hood's Confederates could continue to cause trouble behind Sherman's forces. So Sherman sent 60,000 troops under the command of George Thomas to Tennessee to deal with Hood's army.

Major Events
1864

November
Schofield escapes Confederates at Spring Hill
Confederate loss at Battle of Franklin

December
Army of Tennessee destroyed by Union at Battle of Nashville

What Do You Know!

WHY WOMEN JOINED
A private in the Union army made $13 a month. A poor woman could make only about half this much from sewing or doing laundry. To make more money, some women disguised themselves as men and joined the army.

Spring Hill

Thomas stationed 30,000 troops in Pulaski, Tennessee. This force was under the command of John Schofield. Thomas went with the other 30,000 soldiers under his command to Nashville.

Hood saw an opportunity to defeat the two parts of Thomas's army separately. Hood would defeat Schofield first, then advance on Thomas in Nashville.

Hood tried to march his forces between the two Union camps at Pulaski and Nashville, 75 miles (121 km) to the north. Schofield learned of Hood's advance in time to retreat to Columbia, Tennessee.

The Trap

Encouraged by the Union retreat, Hood sent the cavalry under Nathan Bedford Forrest around Schofield's forces. Its goal was to seize the road behind Schofield at the small town of Spring Hill, Tennessee, located between Columbia and Franklin. With Hood's forces in front and Forrest's in the rear, Hood hoped to trap the Union army. Then his forces could destroy it.

Upon learning of Hood's movements, Thomas ordered Schofield to withdraw from Columbia to Franklin. To get there, the Union forces would have to pass through Spring Hill.

General John Schofield

Opportunity Missed

Schofield sent a small force and most of his **artillery** ahead of the main force. This small force, commanded by David Stanley, reached Spring Hill before the Confederate forces. There, Stanley's men set up strong defenses. On November 29, the Confederates made several attempts to take Spring Hill. Stanley's Union defenders held firm. As darkness fell, the Confederates settled down for the night.

The efforts of Stanley's small Union force had kept the road open. Now the main part of Schofield's army had a path to retreat. While the Confederates slept, Schofield's army marched throughout the night from Columbia through Spring Hill to Franklin. When Hood awoke in the morning, he discovered that Schofield's army had escaped. Hood was furious! He had missed his best chance to defeat the Union army.

The Battle of Franklin

Hood immediately ordered his troops to chase Schofield. They were too late. The Confederates arrived in Franklin the afternoon of November 30. By then, the Union forces had dug in. The earthworks at Franklin were up to eight feet (2 m) high with wide ditches.

The Daring Attack

Hood gathered his commanders together. He ordered them to prepare for a **frontal attack** on the Union earthworks that afternoon. Hood's commanders protested. The Union had strong **fortifications**. They also had many pieces of artillery. Almost all of the Confederate artillery and part of the **infantry** were still traveling toward Franklin. They would not arrive in time for the afternoon battle. Hood did not agree. He had made up his mind.

The Confederates charged across the open ground toward the Union earthworks. They broke through the Union's first line of defense. But their success did not last long. In fierce hand-to-hand fighting, the Union soldiers drove the Confederates back.

The shooting continued well after dark. Near midnight, the Union forces broke off the battle. They marched north to Nashville.

The Battle of Franklin, November 30, 1864

The Result

In spite of the Union's retreat, the battle of Franklin did not result in Confederate victory. Hood lost 7,000 men, three times the Union losses.

Six of Hood's generals lay among the Confederate dead. Six more generals were wounded. Half of all the **regimental** commanders fell dead or were wounded. Those losses dealt a crippling blow to Hood's army. The battle produced another setback for Hood. Schofield's forces had succeeded in uniting with Thomas's forces in Nashville.

The Battle of Nashville

After the battle at Franklin, Hood urged his exhausted troops north toward Nashville, the capital of Tennessee. Winter was approaching, and the Confederate soldiers were ill-equipped for it. They were cold and hungry. Their clothes were ragged. Their shoes were so worn out that some soldiers marched barefoot. Hood knew that the Union held vast stores of supplies in Nashville. If the Confederates could take the city, these supplies would be theirs.

On December 2, 1864, the Confederates arrived outside Nashville. They built defensive earthworks. Then they waited for Thomas's Union army to attack.

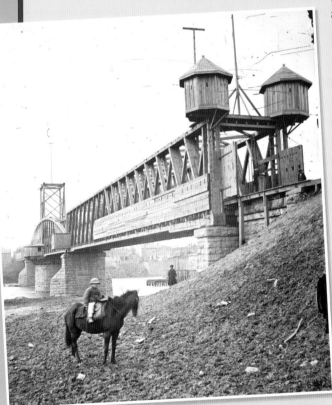

A fortified railroad bridge across the Cumberland River during the Battle of Nashville

A Well-Planned Attack

For the first two weeks in December, Thomas carefully planned his moves. General Grant was becoming impatient. He wondered if Thomas would ever attack. Grant sent a stream of messages to Thomas, ordering him to act. Finally, on December 15, 50,000 Union soldiers surged toward Hood's army of 25,000.

Thomas had crafted a brilliant plan. A Union division, with two brigades of black soldiers, pinned down Hood's right flank. Later, the main Union forces hit hard at Hood's left flank. The Confederates barely held on through the day.

The Destruction of the Army of Tennessee

The next day, December 16, Thomas's forces attacked the flanks again. This time, the Confederate left flank gave way. Hood's army collapsed. Thousands of Confederates surrendered. Many others fled south, dropping their weapons along the way.

The Union cavalry chased the remaining members of Hood's army through Tennessee, Alabama, and Mississippi. By the time the Confederates reached Tupelo, Mississippi, only about half of Hood's army of 40,000 remained.

With his army shattered, General John Hood resigned his command in disgrace. The once-proud Army of Tennessee was a fighting force no more.

People in the War

Jennie Hodgers

Albert Cashier was the shortest soldier in the Union infantry unit. The military did not do physical exams in those days. So no one knew that Albert Cashier was really Jennie Hodgers, a woman.

Hodgers fought bravely in more than 40 battles, including the Battle of Nashville. After the war, Hodgers continued to live as a man. When her secret was discovered, the army tried to take away her veteran's pay. Fellow soldiers rushed to her defense. When she died in 1915, she was buried in her uniform.

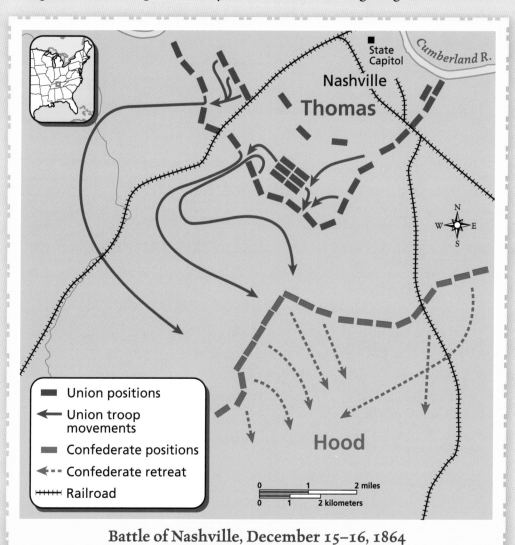

Key:
- Union positions
- Union troop movements
- Confederate positions
- Confederate retreat
- Railroad

Battle of Nashville, December 15–16, 1864

Sherman's Southern Campaign

Major Events

1864

November
Sherman begins his March to the Sea; Atlanta, Georgia, is left in ruins

December
Sherman occupies Savannah, Georgia

1865

January
Sherman begins his march through the Carolinas

February
Sherman occupies Columbia and Charleston, South Carolina

March
Confederate forces withdraw at Battle of Bentonville

Sherman occupies Goldsboro, North Carolina

On September 2, 1864, William Tecumseh Sherman marched his army into Atlanta in triumph. While his troops rested in Atlanta, Sherman hatched a bold plan to bring the South to its knees. When the departing Confederate forces of John Bell Hood retreated toward Tennessee, they had raided Sherman's supply lines. Sherman sent part of his army under General George Thomas to deal with Hood in Tennessee. This freed Sherman's remaining force of 62,000 to carry out the rest of his plan.

Sherman's March to the Sea

All armies need supplies to continue fighting. Southern farms and factories produced food, weapons, and **ammunition**. Although many railroad lines had been destroyed, railroads were still bringing supplies to the Confederate troops. Sherman wanted to destroy all the things that helped the South wage war.

Sherman's plan went beyond military targets. His army would ravage civilian property as well. Sherman knew that Confederate fighters drew strength from the people of the South who believed

> *I can make this march, and make Georgia howl!*
>
> —William Tecumseh Sherman, in a letter to convince Ulysses S. Grant to approve his plan

in the cause. Sherman would wage total war on Georgia. He believed that the suffering Georgians would soon demand an end to the war.

Sherman's plan was to smash through Georgia to Savannah on the Atlantic Ocean. This campaign of destruction would become known as *Sherman's March to the Sea*.

The March Begins

On November 15, 1864, Sherman's men burned Atlanta. They left Atlanta in ruins when they marched out of the city.

Sherman wanted to move quickly. His army would be out of reach of Union supplies during the march. He planned for the soldiers to live off the land. Grant and Lincoln would only know of Sherman's progress from Southern newspapers.

Sherman divided his soldiers into two columns, about 30 miles (48 km) apart. This spread out the soldiers to give them a wider area to **forage**. It also enlarged the army's path of destruction. The soldiers could cover an average of 12 miles (19 km) a day.

Sherman kept his destination a secret. Only Grant, Lincoln, and a few top commanders knew where Sherman was going. To confuse the enemy, Sherman sent one column toward Macon, Georgia. He sent the other column toward Augusta, Georgia. He hoped that the Confederates would send defenders to these two cities. After faking an advance toward Macon and Augusta, the Union columns would continue the march toward Savannah.

Bummers

Groups of Union soldiers scoured the countryside searching for food for the troops. They became known as **bummers**. Bummers raided farms and stole cows, chickens, and hogs. They took any food they could find. Whatever they couldn't carry, they burned.

> ❝
> *I could cut a swath [wide path] through to the sea, divide the Confederacy in two, and be able to move up in the rear of Lee...*
> —William Tecumseh Sherman to General Porter, September 20, 1864
> ❞

🌀 What Do You Know!

THE TELEGRAPH
Abraham Lincoln was the first president who could communicate instantly with his officers on the battlefield. The telegraph made this possible. In 1862, the U.S. Military Telegraph Corps strung 4,000 miles (6,437 km) of telegraph wire. More than a million messages passed to and from the Union lines. The Confederacy lacked the technology to create such a large communications network.

Union commanders had little control over the bummers. Looting became profitable. Most of Georgia's men were off fighting. Their wives tried to save their silver and jewelry by burying them. The bummers poked into the freshly dug earth in flower beds to uncover the treasure.

Not all bummers were Union soldiers. Confederate **deserters** and freed slaves also foraged in the Georgia countryside.

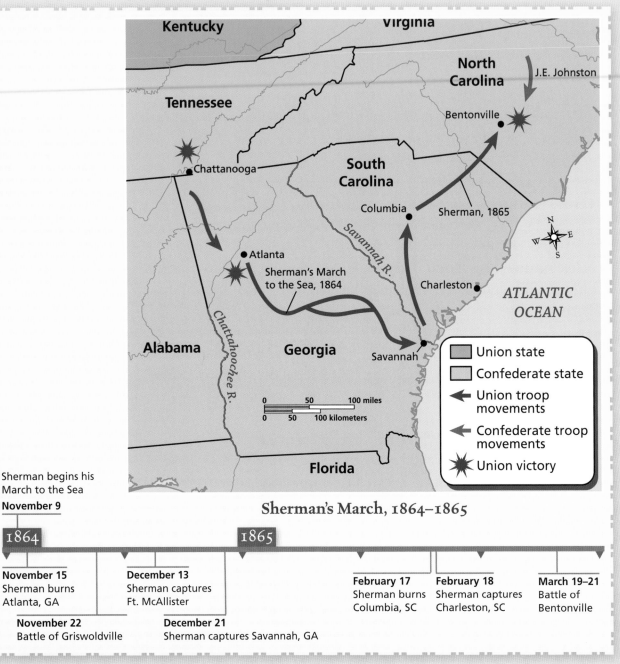

Sherman's March, 1864–1865

Sherman begins his
March to the Sea
November 9

1864　　　　　　**1865**

November 15
Sherman burns
Atlanta, GA

November 22
Battle of Griswoldville

December 13
Sherman captures
Ft. McAllister

December 21
Sherman captures Savannah, GA

February 17
Sherman burns
Columbia, SC

February 18
Sherman captures
Charleston, SC

March 19–21
Battle of
Bentonville

Map labels: Kentucky, Virginia, North Carolina, J.E. Johnston, Tennessee, Bentonville, Chattanooga, South Carolina, Columbia, Sherman, 1865, Savannah R., Atlanta, Sherman's March to the Sea, 1864, Charleston, ATLANTIC OCEAN, Alabama, Georgia, Savannah, Chattahoochee R., Florida

Legend:
Union state
Confederate state
Union troop movements
Confederate troop movements
Union victory

Scale: 0　50　100 miles
0　50　100 kilometers

Freed Slaves on the March

As Sherman's army swept through Georgia, the slaves in the area found themselves suddenly free. Many traveled along behind Sherman's columns. Grant suggested that Sherman recruit freed slaves as soldiers. Sherman did not do this.

Sherman tried to stop these **refugees** from following his troops. To Sherman, they were extra mouths to feed. Still, the refugees kept coming.

Skirmish at Griswoldville

Sherman's men met little opposition on their march. Only the Georgia militia and a small cavalry stood in the way. On November 22, the Georgia militia attacked the Union column at Griswoldville, just outside of Macon, Georgia. The Confederates charged several times. Each time, the Union forces cut them down. The militia lost more than 600 soldiers, compared to the Union's 62.

Celebration changed to horror when the Union soldiers viewed the battlefield. For the first time, they realized that they had been fighting young boys and old men.

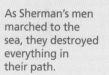

As Sherman's men marched to the sea, they destroyed everything in their path.

Fort McAllister

Sherman's army pushed ever deeper into Georgia, destroying railroad tracks, warehouses, factories, and cotton gins. Like a swarm of insects, they consumed everything.

On December 9, 1864, Sherman's troops arrived outside of Savannah. They had marched without pause for four weeks. In that time, they had cut a path of destruction as much as 60 miles (97 km) wide and 285 miles (459 km) long.

> " *The destruction could hardly have been worse, if Atlanta had been a volcano in eruption and the molten lava had flowed in a stream sixty miles wide and five times as long.* "
>
> —Union soldier, recalling Sherman's March to the Sea

29

After capturing Ft. McAllister, Sherman's men removed its big guns.

Savannah's main defense was Fort McAllister. It stood on the bank of the Ogeechee River, with a view of the Atlantic Ocean. Sherman decided to take the fort to clear the waterway to Savannah. Only 250 Confederates held the fort. On December 13, Sherman's men attacked. They overwhelmed the defenders within 15 minutes. Sherman had reached the sea.

Union ships were waiting for Sherman's arrival. With Fort McAllister under Union control, the ships steamed up the river unopposed. They brought **rations** and letters. It was the first mail the soldiers received since the march began.

Savannah

A force of only about 10,000 Confederates guarded Savannah. They had little hope of defeating Sherman's force of 60,000. Sherman sent a message to the Confederate commander, William Hardee. Sherman offered Hardee a chance to surrender. Hardee refused.

Part of Hardee's army had been protecting an escape route out of the city. To save his army, Hardee ordered his soldiers to evacuate. On December 21, Sherman's army marched into Savannah without a fight.

At about the same time, President Lincoln received good news from Tennessee. On December 16, Union forces under George Thomas captured Nashville. They had destroyed the Confederate army of John Bell Hood. News of the disasters in Georgia and Tennessee spread despair through the South.

> *I beg to present to you as a Christmas gift the City of Savannah…*
>
> —William Tecumseh Sherman, telegraph message to President Lincoln, December 22, 1864

Sherman in the Carolinas

The Union army rested in Savannah until mid-January 1865. Then Sherman began the second part of his plan. His army would slash and burn through the Carolinas. The goal was to emerge behind the army of Robert E. Lee at Petersburg,

> *The truth is the whole army is burning with [a] desire to wreak vengeance [revenge] upon South Carolina. I almost tremble for her fate, but feel that she deserves all that seems in store for her.*
>
> —William Tecumseh Sherman, letter to General Henry Halleck, December 24, 1864

near Richmond. This would trap the Confederates between Grant's and Sherman's armies. Together, the Union armies could crush the mighty Army of Northern Virginia.

Sherman and his soldiers also had another purpose. South Carolina was the first state to secede. The war began at Fort Sumter in the harbor of Charleston, South Carolina. Sherman's men blamed the state for starting the terrible war. They wanted to punish South Carolina.

Battling the Elements

The march into South Carolina presented challenges for the Union soldiers. The winter weather was unusually wet. They had to cross rivers and swamps that were swollen with rainwater. Many roads were under water. The soldiers sometimes waded in water that was chest deep.

Sherman organized soldiers and freed slaves into groups he called **pioneer battalions**. They cut trees to build roads and bridges. These structures enabled the wagons and artillery to pass. Despite the terrible weather and rugged **terrain**, Sherman's army managed to travel ten miles (16 km) a day.

The Burning of Columbia

Sherman divided his soldiers into two columns as he had done during the march through Georgia. One column pointed toward Augusta, Georgia. The other pointed toward Charleston, South Carolina. The Confederates could not tell which city Sherman would attack. Sherman's army, however, was really headed for Columbia, South Carolina.

With no hope of defending Columbia against such a strong enemy, the Confederates evacuated the city. On February 17, 1865, Sherman's army marched into Columbia. His soldiers unleashed their full fury on the city. That night, flames lit up the sky.

Charleston

On February 18, 1865, part of Sherman's army approached the outskirts of Charleston, South Carolina. The small force of Confederate defenders fled the city.

Union forces now occupied the "cradle of the Confederacy"—the city where secession began. Among the first to enter Charleston were the black soldiers of the 55th Massachusetts Infantry.

Battle of Bentonville

After a few days in Columbia, Sherman's troops were again on the march, and again in two columns. The Confederates could only guess where Sherman was going. By mid-March, his target had become clear. It was Goldsboro, a railroad center in North Carolina.

In January, Fort Fisher had fallen to General Schofield's Union army. The fort had guarded the city of Wilmington, on the North Carolina coast. The capture of Wilmington closed the South's last major **seaport**.

Ruined buildings in Charleston, South Carolina

Schofield's orders were to march inland from Wilmington with supplies for Sherman's army. The two armies would meet and join forces at Goldsboro.

On February 22, Jefferson Davis put Joseph Johnston in charge of all Confederate forces in the Carolinas. Johnston combined the forces from Charleston, Augusta, and Savannah. He also picked up some scattered remaining members of Hood's army. Johnston had a force of about 20,000.

Johnston gathered his forces at Bentonville, North Carolina. He hoped to **ambush** one column of Sherman's army before the two columns could reunite. Meanwhile, Sherman believed that Johnston would send his forces to defend Raleigh, North Carolina.

On March 19, the Union column walked into Johnston's trap. All day, the Confederate forces bore down on the surprised Union soldiers. By the end of the day, the Union force was badly bruised but not broken. Sherman sent reinforcements. By the next day, the Union forces seriously outnumbered Johnston's forces. Johnston had no choice but to slip away in the night. The Battle of Bentonville marked the end of major fighting in North Carolina.

Goldsboro

Sherman rode into Goldsboro on March 23. His soldiers had traveled 425 miles (684 km) from Savannah. For 45 days, they had slogged across mud-filled roads, swamps, and swift-flowing rivers.

Schofield was waiting in Goldsboro with supplies and men to restock Sherman's army. With Schofield's army, Sherman now had a force of 89,000. Johnston could do little to stop this powerful army from advancing into Virginia. If Sherman could combine with Grant near Richmond, as planned, Robert E. Lee would face a total Union force of 217,000!

Effects of Sherman's Campaign

Sherman brought misery and fear to the heart of the Confederacy. The people of Georgia and the Carolinas realized that their government could not protect them. Many lost hope of winning the war. They wanted the fighting to end.

The destruction also hurt the Confederate soldiers. Sherman's troops destroyed supplies and supply routes through the South. The Confederate soldiers also heard the cries of their families back home. Many soldiers deserted to go home to protect their families. Sherman's campaign through Georgia and the Carolinas probably helped to end the war more quickly.

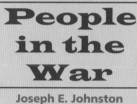

People in the War

Joseph E. Johnston

Joseph Johnston graduated from West Point military academy. When his home state of Virginia seceded, Johnston became the highest ranking officer to resign from the U.S. Army.

As a Confederate officer, Johnston often clashed with Jefferson Davis. Davis took away his command because he thought Johnston acted too cautiously. Only with persuasion from Robert E. Lee did Davis return Johnston to command in the Carolinas. Johnston was soon forced to surrender to his rival, William Tecumseh Sherman.

After the war, Johnston and Sherman became friends. Johnston died in 1891. He had caught pneumonia while serving as a pallbearer at Sherman's funeral.

The Civil War Ends

Major Events

1864

May 5–June 9
Overland Campaign

May 5–September 2
Atlanta Campaign

June 9–April 2
Petersburg siege

August 5
Mobile Bay

August 6–October 19
Sheridan in Shenandoah

November 8
Lincoln reelected

November 15–December 21
Sherman's March to the Sea

1865

January 15–March 23
Carolina Campaign

February 17
Columbia burned

April 3
Richmond falls

April 9
Lee surrenders

April 15
Lincoln assassinated

April 26
Johnston surrenders

By the time Sherman entered Goldsboro on March 23, 1865, Petersburg, Virginia, had been under siege for about nine months. Both Grant and Lee knew the value of Petersburg. It was a center of industry. Five railroads and several plank roads ran through the city. They brought supplies to Confederate forces in the field. If Petersburg fell, there would be nothing to stop Union forces from taking nearby Richmond, the Confederate capital.

Grant's Army of the Potomac had been entrenched outside the city since June 1864. Lee's Army of Northern Virginia was determined to hold the city.

The Noose Tightens on Petersburg

Throughout the fall and winter of 1864, Grant's forces raided Confederate supply lines. They captured roads, bridges, and railroads around Petersburg. They succeeded in stopping the flow of supplies to Lee's army. The Confederates were cold and starving. The soldiers' spirits dropped. Many deserted. Lee's army of 55,000 was shrinking.

Meanwhile, Grant's army of 90,000 was well stocked. Grant established a supply base at City Point, a few miles (km) from Petersburg. Union troops built eight **wharves** along the banks of the James River. Boats brought supplies each day. Grant directed the activities of all the Union armies from his headquarters at City Point.

Throughout the siege, Grant expanded his lines around Petersburg. This forced Lee to stretch his outnumbered army. By March 1865, both sides knew the end was near. Grant expected Sherman's army to arrive by late April. The combined armies of Grant and Sherman could surely overwhelm Lee's army in Petersburg.

Fort Stedman

Meanwhile, Lee plotted a way to break out of the noose. He realized that his army had to leave Petersburg and allow Richmond to fall. This was the only way to prevent the destruction of his army.

Lee and General John B. Gordon planned a surprise attack on Fort Stedman, east of Petersburg. Victory there would open an escape route. It would also place the Confederates close enough to City Point to threaten Union headquarters. Once Lee's troops were clear of Petersburg, they would

Union supplies were brought ashore at City Point near Petersburg. City Point was General Grant's headquarters during the seige of Petersburg.

march to join Joseph Johnston's army in North Carolina. Together, the two armies could attack Sherman before he could unite with Grant.

Lee massed his troops for the attack. Gordon's force of 12,000 would lead the charge.

Just before dawn on March 25, 1865, a group of Confederate soldiers quietly cleared away obstacles. Meanwhile, a few Confederates pretended to be deserters. They approached the Union guards and began a conversation. When they were close enough, the Confederates quickly captured the surprised guards.

Gordon gave the signal, and the first wave of soldiers swept through the clearing. They wore strips of white cloth across their chests so their companions could see them in the dark. Under the blasts of Union cannons, the Confederates swarmed over the walls and took the fort.

The Confederates now had control of the fort's big guns. They turned the guns on the Union earthworks on both sides of the fort. They soon captured a half-mile (1 km) of Union trenches. Gordon's forces seemed to have achieved the breakthrough that Lee wanted.

People in the War

**James Longstreet
Confederate General**

"My Old War Horse," Robert E. Lee called his trusted friend, James Longstreet. Indeed, Longstreet was a veteran of many battles by the time he fought with Lee at Petersburg.

Longstreet attended West Point military academy. There, he struck up a friendship with a young man named Ulysses S. Grant. Longstreet even served as best man at Grant's wedding.

As Longstreet watched the battle at Fort Gregg, he recognized his old friend Grant. Longstreet did not know at the time that in one week, the two would be countrymen again.

The battle was not over. Heavy Union fire erupted around Fort Stedman. The Confederates in the fort were trapped. By the end of the day, Union forces had retaken the fort. Many Confederates surrendered.

Lee lost about 5,000 men, while Grant lost just 2,000. The loss of so many Confederate soldiers reduced the chances for Lee's army to survive.

Five Forks

Grant knew that the failed attack at Fort Stedman had weakened Lee's lines. Grant thought he could break through without waiting for Sherman to arrive. Grant seized the opportunity to strike.

Philip Sheridan's cavalry had recently arrived from the Shenandoah Valley. Grant sent Sheridan's forces around the side of Lee's lines southwest of Petersburg. Lee sent forces under George Pickett to stop Sheridan.

The crossroads known as Five Forks was crucial to Lee. The Southside Railroad near the crossroads was the last supply line for Lee's forces in Petersburg. Lee ordered Pickett to protect Five Forks "at all hazards [costs]."

At first, Pickett succeeded in slowing the Union advance. Sheridan launched a spirited attack at Five Forks on April 1, 1865. Sheridan stormed along his lines, urging his men on. Pickett's forces collapsed. More than 5,000 were captured.

The Union now controlled Southside Railroad line. Sheridan's cavalry was also in position to cut off Lee's line of retreat. Lee knew his army had to get out fast.

The Breakthrough at Petersburg

Grant saw his opportunity to end the siege in victory. He immediately ordered an all-out attack for the next day, April 2. Before dawn, Union forces would strike along the entire Confederate line.

At midnight, Union artillery began blasting the Confederate earthworks. Around 4:00 A.M., the Union infantry surged forward. They tore through the sharp stakes and rain-filled ditches protecting the Confederate lines. Then they poured into the trenches. Much of the fighting was hand-to-hand. Soon word reached Lee that Grant's forces had broken through.

To escape, Lee's army had to cross the bridge over the Appomattox River. A small Confederate force at Fort Gregg and Fort Whitworth protected the escape route. Lee ordered General James Longstreet to bring his men to protect the retreat. The defenders at the two forts had to hold out long enough for Longstreet's forces to arrive.

The Confederates at Fort Gregg faced a Union force ten times their size. The tired, hungry Southerners fought desperately. They refused to surrender. Finally, the Union soldiers overwhelmed them. Of the 300 Confederates inside Fort Gregg, about 270 lay dead or wounded.

The **heroic** stand by the men of Fort Gregg bought the time Lee needed. Longstreet's forces were able to prevent Grant's army from completing the circle around Lee. When the fighting stopped for the night, Lee's army slipped across the Appomattox River.

After a ten-month stalemate, Petersburg fell into Union hands. Now nothing stood between Grant and Richmond.

Fall of Richmond

April 2, 1865, was a Sunday. Jefferson Davis was attending a church service in Richmond when a messenger approached. He brought a telegram from General Lee. The Confederate government must evacuate Richmond.

Panic spread through the city. Davis and other government officials gathered what they could and boarded trains to Danville, Virginia. Citizens scrambled to leave by whatever means they could. Before the

Ruins of Richmond, Virginia, 1865

> *I advise that all preparation be made for leaving Richmond tonight.*
>
> —General Lee's telegram to President Jefferson Davis

Confederate soldiers left that night, they set fire to everything of military value in Richmond. Mills and warehouses burned. Stored ammunition exploded in the heat of the fire. Flames spread through the city. Frightened people huddled wherever they could find shelter.

The next morning, Union forces entered Richmond without a fight. Among the first to arrive was the 25th Corps. This unit of black soldiers worked to put out the flames and restore order to the city. By nightfall, fire had consumed more than 700 buildings.

When Richmond fell, Abraham Lincoln was at Union headquarters at City Point. On April 4, Lincoln traveled up the James River on a navy ship to visit the Confederate capital. As Lincoln toured the city, joyful former slaves surrounded him. They were finally free.

Appomattox Campaign

Lee's army retreated from Richmond toward Danville. There, Lee hoped to join with Johnson's army coming from North Carolina. Together, the two armies could attack Sherman's forces.

Grant was determined to stop Lee from reaching Johnston. As soon as Richmond fell, Grant sent Sheridan's cavalry and several infantry units after Lee's retreating army.

Amelia Court House

By this time, only 35,000 soldiers remained in Lee's army. They were weary and starving. The retreating forces from Petersburg and Richmond met at the town of Amelia Court House. They expected to find a trainload of rations sent from Richmond, but the rations did not arrive.

Lee knew that they had to move fast. Still, his hungry soldiers could not march without food. They had to stop and forage in the countryside. Farmers had little to give. The forage wagons returned without enough food to feed the army.

The delay proved **critical**. While Lee's troops foraged, Sheridan's horsemen had time to catch up.

Lee's forces left Amelia Court House on April 5. In only a few miles (km) they found Union soldiers blocking their way. Rather than fight, Lee turned his army west toward Farmville, Virginia.

Battle of Sailor's Creek

Union troops jabbed constantly at the fleeing Confederates. Hundreds of exhausted Southern soldiers collapsed by the roadside. Gaps began to form in Confederate lines.

At Sailor's Creek, near Farmville, the Union cavalry rushed through one of these gaps. This cut off one-quarter of Lee's army. About 6,000 Confederates were captured. About 2,000 more were killed or wounded. Lee's army was nearly gone.

Battle of Appomattox Court House

Lee changed direction and continued the retreat. Each time Lee turned, Union troops soon blocked his path.

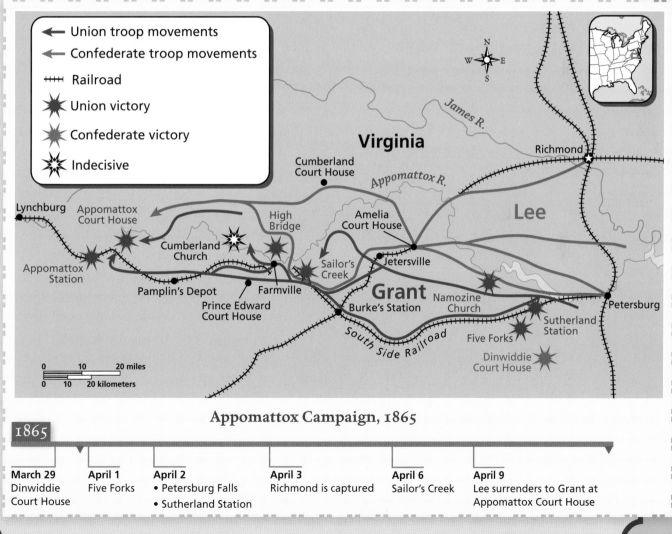

Appomattox Campaign, 1865

1865

March 29	April 1	April 2	April 3	April 6	April 9
Dinwiddie Court House	Five Forks	• Petersburg Falls • Sutherland Station	Richmond is captured	Sailor's Creek	Lee surrenders to Grant at Appomattox Court House

> *Then there is nothing left for me to do but go and see General Grant, and I would rather die a thousand deaths.*
>
> —Robert E. Lee to his staff, Appomattox Courthouse, Virginia, April 9, 1865

On April 7, Grant sent a message asking Lee to surrender but Lee was not yet ready to give up the fight. If his forces could reach the town of Appomattox Court House, they might still escape. To get there, though, they would have to break through Sheridan's force that was blocking the way.

In one last desperate action, the Confederates charged the Union lines. But the Union forces far outnumbered the Confederates. Meanwhile, more Union troops moved in behind Lee. The Confederates were trapped. Lee had no choice. He had to surrender.

Surrender at Appomattox Court House

On April 9, 1865, Lee and Grant met at the home of Wilmer McLean in Appomattox Court House. Lee arrived in his dress uniform. Grant appeared in mud-spattered pants.

Grant offered easy terms of surrender. He was following Lincoln's wish to unite the nation, not punish the South. Grant promised Lee that the Confederate soldiers would not be tried for treason. They just had to lay down their weapons and promise not to continue the fight. Then they could go home in peace.

The two great leaders signed the surrender papers and shook hands. As Lee left, Grant tipped his hat to Lee. Lee returned the respectful salute and sadly rode toward his waiting troops.

Upon receiving the news, Union troops celebrated with cheers and rifle shots into the air. Grant ordered them to stop. They should not rejoice in the defeat of their enemy, he explained. Instead, they should welcome the Southerners back as countrymen. Grant sent rations to the starving Confederate soldiers. When the Confederate soldiers laid down their weapons, the Union soldiers lowered their rifles as a sign of respect.

Lee surrendered to Grant in the home of Wilmer McLean at Appomattox Court House.

The End of the Confederacy

For most Americans on both sides, Lee's surrender to Grant marked the end of the Civil War. Yet forces remained in the field. Also, Jefferson Davis had escaped.

Remaining Forces Surrender

At his headquarters in Raleigh, North Carolina, Sherman received word of Lee's surrender. Sherman sent a message to Johnston at his headquarters in nearby Hillsboro, North Carolina. He invited Johnston to meet to discuss surrender.

On April 26, 1865, Johnston met Sherman at Durham Station, North Carolina. Sherman offered Johnston the same easy terms that Grant offered Lee. Johnston surrendered 89,270 soldiers. This was the largest single surrender of the war.

On May 4, 1865, Confederate General Richard Taylor surrendered to Union General Edward Canby at Citronelle, Alabama. This was the last Confederate force east of the Mississippi River to lay down its weapons.

Scattered Confederate troops still remained west of the Mississippi. The final skirmish of the war occurred at Palmito Ranch, Texas. On May 26, 1865, General E.K. Smith surrendered his Trans-Mississippi forces at New Orleans, Louisiana.

What Do You Know!

McLEAN HOUSE
In 1861, Wilmer McLean was living near Manassas, Virginia, when a Union shell crashed into his house. To escape the fighting, McLean moved his family to the sleepy village of Appomattox Court House.

In April 1865, the war found him again. The top generals of the opposing armies sat in his parlor. This time, they were talking peace.

Jefferson Davis Captured

President Jefferson Davis had been on the run since he and the rest of the Confederate government evacuated Richmond. The government relocated to Danville, Virginia. Soon they had to move farther south. After leaving Danville, the Confederate government disbanded.

Jefferson Davis continued to flee south with Union forces on his heels. On May 9, Davis and his family made camp at the small community of Irwinville, Georgia. When they awoke on the morning of May 10, they found Union troops surrounding them. Davis was captured. He would remain in prison for two years.

Assassination of Abraham Lincoln

Sadly, Abraham Lincoln would not live to see the end of the war. An **assassin's** bullet took his life.

John Wilkes Booth, an actor, believed strongly in the Confederate cause. Soon after Lee's surrender, Booth hatched a plan that he thought would save the Confederacy.

On April 14, 1865, Lincoln and his wife attended a play at Ford's Theatre in Washington, DC, Booth slipped into the president's private box. He shot Lincoln in the back of the head. Booth leapt onto the stage, shouted a Confederate **slogan**, and escaped. Lincoln was carried to a house across the street. The next morning, Lincoln died. Less than two weeks later, Booth was caught and killed.

A train carrying Lincoln's body made its way slowly from Washington to Lincoln's hometown of Springfield, Illinois. All along the route, people gathered to mourn.

Summary of the Final Campaigns

In the spring of 1864, the Civil War entered its final stages. Grant directed the movements of the Union armies to achieve final victory.

During the Overland Campaign, Grant's army fought Lee's army through the bloody battles of the Wilderness, Spotsylvania, and Cold Harbor. In June 1864, Grant pinned Lee down in Petersburg in a siege that would last ten long months. Meanwhile, Sherman's march through Tennessee halted outside of Atlanta. With both Sherman and Grant stalled, public opinion in the North turned against the war. Lincoln's chances for reelection looked dim.

Three major successes in the fall of 1864 came just in time for Lincoln. Sheridan nearly destroyed Jubal Early's Confederate army in the Shenandoah Valley. At the same time, David Farragut captured Mobile Bay. This prevented the Confederates from receiving supplies through this port. Less than two weeks later, Atlanta fell to Sherman's troops. Seeing final victory at hand, Northern voters reelected Lincoln.

After leaving Atlanta, Hood retreated into Tennessee. Schofield followed him. After the battle of Franklin, Schofield's troops destroyed Hood's army at Nashville.

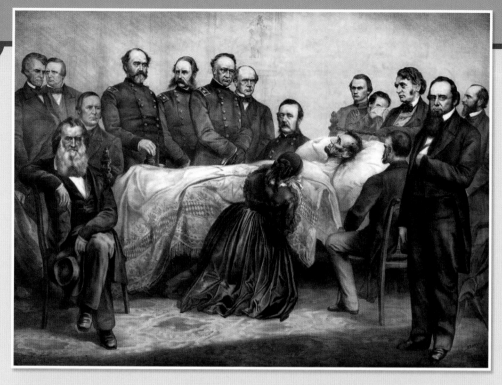

President Abraham Lincoln on his deathbed, April 1865

Meanwhile, Sherman brought total war to the heart of the Confederacy. His troops smashed through Georgia and the Carolinas, destroying everything in their path. By February 1865, the cities of Atlanta, Columbia, and Charleston lay in ruins. The destruction wore down the will of Southerners to continue fighting.

Finally, the breakthrough at Petersburg led to the fall of Richmond. Lee surrendered at Appomattox on April 9, 1865. The remaining Confederate forces soon gave up. The long, bloody war was over.

Effects of the Civil War

The cost of the war in human lives and destruction was shocking. No less astonishing were the effects on society.

Human Cost

About three million soldiers fought in the Civil War. More than 620,000 of them lost their lives. About 470,000 more were wounded. Many had lost arms or legs. One out of ten able-bodied men from the North was dead or injured. For the South, the number was one out of four.

Human suffering extended to civilians as well. Thousands of Southerners lost their homes and possessions. Families on both sides had to deal with the loss of husbands, brothers, and sons.

Economic Cost

The war destroyed the economy of the South. Railroads and industries were destroyed. Farms and farm machinery were ruined. Foragers had taken livestock and food crops. Farmers in the South had depended on slave labor. That source of labor was gone.

The Northern economy had not suffered as much. Most of the destruction had occurred in the South.

Social Changes

The outcome of the war brought an end to the idea of **secession**. The United States would be one nation, not two. The bitterness between the people of the North and South, however, would continue long after the war.

Union victory ended slavery throughout the country. Former slaves became citizens when the Thirteenth Amendment became part of the Constitution on December 18, 1865. The question then facing the nation was how to blend African Americans into society. They lacked homes and jobs. Many whites in the South and the North still viewed African Americans as **inferior**. **Prejudice** would continue to deny African Americans full rights as citizens.

The outcome of the Civil War set the nation on a new course, but the road to recovery would be long and difficult.

GLOSSARY

ambush A surprise attack from a concealed position

ammunition Rifle bullets, gunpowder, and/or shells to be used in artillery guns, rifles, or pistols

artillery Large guns that are usually mounted on a carriage so they can be moved from place to place and fired a long distance at enemy positions

assassin A person who plots and carries out a murder, often of a political figure

blockade To use hostile ships to close off trade

blockade runner Fast, light ship that could slip past the Union blockade to transport goods to and from the Confederate states

bummers Unruly Union soldiers who raided civilian farms and homes in their search for food and valuable items

casualties A loss in the fighting strength of a military unit due to causes such as wounds or death

civilian A person who is not a member of the military or involved in fighting

coordinate To plan the movement or operations of one military force in relation to another to accomplish a goal

counterattack An attack that is made in reaction to a previous attack

critical Something that is essential or very important; involving risk

deserter A member of the military who runs away without permission

despair A sense of hopelessness

discontent Dissatisfaction with one's condition and a desire for change

earthworks Defensive structures around a military position made with mounds of earth

engage To attack an enemy force

entrenched When an armed force is set in a defensive position in trenches or behind objects that will shield it from enemy fire

flank The right or left side of the position of a military force

forage To look for food and supplies often by looting the homes and farms of civilians

fortifications The defensive structures around a city, town, or fort that may include walls, earth mounds, or trenches

frontal attack A direct attack on the front line of the defensive position of an enemy

hand-to-hand Close up fighting between enemies

heroic Admirable actions that are brave and selfless

humiliating Causing a sense of shame or dishonor

independence Acting freely; no longer under the control of others

infantry Soldiers who fight on foot and carry their own supplies and weapons

Glossary

inferior Something of low quality; not up to a standard

ironclad A ship covered with iron plates for protection from enemy fire

mast A pole rising above a ship that holds sails and rigging

necessities Basic or essential items, such as food and water

negotiations Talks about issues before an agreement

pioneer battalion Group of Union soldiers and freed slaves who cut trees and built roads and bridges during Sherman's March to the Sea

plank road A dirt path covered with wooden planks to make it easier for wagons, horses, and people to use

platform A statement of the beliefs of a political candidate or party

prejudice A negative opinion or prejudgment about a person or situation; a conclusion reached without sufficient thought

promote To advance in rank to a higher position

rations A fixed amount of food provided to civilians or military personnel

refugee A person who leaves home as a result of war

regimental Relating to a regiment, which is a unit made up of about 1,000 men within the army

reinforce To provide additional men and weapons to add strength to an existing military force

resources The sources of supplies, such as farms and factories, that can aid the war effort

routed A disorganized retreat resulting from a military force being driven from its position by an enemy

seaport A city or town with a harbor on the seacoast

secession The withdrawal of Southern states from the United States to set up a separate nation called the Confederate States of America

siege The isolation of a hostile city or town to deprive the people within it of food, water, and other essential supplies

skirmish A brief conflict between troops

slogan A phrase or motto of an individual or group

stalemate A deadlock in which no progress can be made on either side

strategy Plans for conducting warfare, including the movement of armed forces in relation to an enemy

terrain The natural features of an area of land

total war Actions in war that destroy not only enemy military forces but also the cities, farms, factories, and civilians that support them

vital A thing that is essential and of great importance

wharf A dock or deck often made of wood that serves as a place for boats or ships to tie up and unload cargo or passengers

MORE INFORMATION

Books

Blaisdell, Bob, editor. *The Civil War: A Book of Quotations.* Dover Publications, 2004.

Foote, Shelby. *The Civil War: A Narrative, Red River to Appomattox.* Random House, 1974.

Horn, Geoffrey M. *Sojourner Truth: Speaking Up for Freedom.* Crabtree Publishing Company, 2010.

McPherson, James M. *The Illustrated Battle Cry of Freedom: The Civil War Era.* Oxford University Press, 2003.

Ward, Geoffrey C. *The Civil War: An Illustrated History.* Alfred A. Knopf, 1992.

Websites

www.pbs.org/civilwar
The Civil War/PBS. Companion site to Ken Burns's DVD *The Civil War.* Includes photos, maps, and video clips.

http://www.nps.gov/civilwar150/
National Park Service Web Site. In-depth articles, photos, and information on Civil War parks and park events.

http://www.history.com/topics/american-civil-war
Articles, photos, and profiles of major Civil War figures.

www.civilwar.org/education/students/kidswebsites.html
Civil War Trust websites for Kids. Has articles, photos, a glossary of Civil War terms, lists of books, and links to other websites.

www.civil-war.net
The Civil War Home Page. Has a photo gallery, lists of books and movies, battle maps, articles, diary excerpts, and reference materials.

http://www.archives.gov/research/military/civil-war/photos/index.html
The National Archives, Pictures of the Civil War.

About the Author

Cinci Stowell has been developing educational materials for more than 30 years. Her writing credits span a range of K–12 subjects, including history, government, economics, geography, and business. Cinci holds a bachelor's degree in English and a master's degree in business.

INDEX

Amelia Court House, 38, 39
Amendment, Thirteenth, 44
Appomattox Campaign, 38–40
Arlington National Cemetery, 18
Army of Northern Virginia, 6, 11, 21, 34
Army of the Potomac, 6, 8, 11, 13, 14, 15, 34
Army of the Shenandoah, 17, 18
Army of Tennessee, 21, 25
artillery, 22, 23, 31, 36
Atlanta Campaign, 9, 10, 12–14, 20, 21, 26–29, 42–43

Banks, Nathaniel P., 7–9, 13
Beauregard, P.G.T., 8
Bentonville, Battle of, 10, 28, 32, 33
Bermuda Hundred, 8
blockade, 19
blockade runners, 19
Booth, John Wilkes, 42
bummers, 27, 28
Butler, Benjamin, 7–9, 13

Canby, Edward, 41
casualties, 11, 16, 24, 43
Cedar Creek, Battle of, 18
Charleston, South Carolina, 10, 18, 28, 31, 32, 43
Chattanooga Campaign, 5–7, 12, 21, 28
City Point, Virginia, 34, 35
Cold Harbor, Battle of, 10, 11, 14, 15, 42
Columbia, South Carolina, 28, 31, 32, 43
Crater, Battle of, 16

Davis, Jefferson, 12, 32, 33, 37, 41
Democratic Party, 14
deserters, 28, 35
Dinwiddie Court House, Battle of, 39

Early, Jubal, 14, 17, 18, 42
earthworks, 15, 23, 24, 35, 36
economic effects of war, 44
Election of 1864, 7, 13, 14, 15, 20, 42

Farragut, David, 19, 20, 43
Five Forks, Battle of, 36, 39
forage, 18, 27, 28, 38, 44
Forrest, Nathan Bedford, 22
Fort Gregg, 36, 37
Fort McAllister, 28–30

Fort Stedman, 35
Fort Sumter, 31
fortifications, 23, 24
Franklin, Battle of, 10, 23, 24, 43

Gordon, John B., 35
Grant, Ulysses S., 6–9, 11-15, 17, 18, 21, 24, 26, 27, 29, 31, 33–42
    and Appomattox Campaign, 38–40
    and Overland Campaign, 9
    at Petersburg, 14, 15
    strategies of, 6, 7
Griswoldville, Battle of, 28, 29

hand-to-hand fighting, 11, 23, 36
Hardee, William J., 30
Hodgers, Jennie, 25
Hood, John Bell, 9, 12, 13, 20–26, 30, 32, 43
Hunter, David, 17

independence, Southern, 7, 14
ironclads, 19, 20

Johnston, Joseph E., 6–9, 12, 28, 32, 33, 35, 38, 41, 43

Lee, Robert E., 6–11, 14, 17, 18, 21, 27, 30, 33–43
    and Appomattox Campaign, 38–40
    and Petersburg, 34–37
Lincoln, Abraham, 6, 7, 13, 14, 17, 20, 27, 30, 38, 40, 42, 43
    assassination of, 42, 43
    reelection of, 13, 14, 20
Longstreet, James, 36, 37
Lynchburg, Virginia, 17, 39

Mansfield, Battle of, 7, 8
McClellan, George B., 14, 20
McLean House, 40, 41
Meade, George, 6–9
Mississippi River, 5, 10, 41
Mobile Bay, Battle of, 10, 19, 20, 42, 43
Monocacy, Battle of, 17

Nashville, Battle of, 10, 24, 25, 30, 43
New Market, Battle of, 5, 8, 17

Overland Campaign, 5, 8, 9, 13, 34, 42

Petersburg Campaign, 8–11, 13–17, 30, 34–39, 42, 43
pioneer battalions, 31
plank roads, 15, 34
Porter, David Dixon, 7

Red River Campaign, 7–9
refugees, 29
resources, war, 6, 12
Richmond, Virginia, 8–11, 14, 31, 33–35, 37–39, 41, 43

Sailor's Creek, Battle of, 39
Savannah, Georgia, 10, 27–29, 30–33
Schofield, John, 22–24, 32, 33, 43
secession, 32, 44
Shenandoah Valley, 8, 17, 18, 20, 36, 42
    and The Burning, 18
Sheridan, Philip, 17, 18, 36, 38, 40
Sherman, William T., 5-7, 9, 10, 12–14, 20, 21, 26-33, 34–36, 38, 41–43
    in the Carolinas, 31–33
    and March to the Sea, 10, 26, 27, 28, 43
Shreveport, Louisiana, 7, 8
Sigel, Franz, 7–9, 13, 17
slavery, 44
slaves, 28, 29, 31, 38, 44
Smith, E.K., 41
social effects of war, 44
Spotsylvania, Battle of, 10, 11, 42
Spring Hill, Battle of, 22
Stanley, David, 22
strategy, Northern, 6, 7, 12, 13
strategy, Southern, 7

Taylor, Richard, 41
telegraph, 27, 30
Thomas, George H., 21, 22, 24–26, 30

Vicksburg Campaign, 5, 6
Virginia Military Institute, 8

Wallace, Lew, 17
Wilderness, Battle of, 9–11, 42
Wilmington, Battle of, 10, 32
women, in war, 21